Keep Yourself Safe

Being Safe
on a Bike

Honor Head

FRANKLIN WATTS
LONDON • SYDNEY

Franklin Watts
First published in Great Britain in 2015 by The Watts Publishing Group

Picture Credits: Cover © Christopher Futcher/iStock; 1, 17 bottom
© Sergey Novikov/Shutterstock; 4 © RonGreer/Shutterstock;
5 © Dmitry Naumov/Shutterstock; 6 © Dean Mitchell/iStock;
8 © S Oleg/Shutterstock; 9 © Aliaksei Smalenski/Shutterstock;
10 © Monkey Business Images/Shutterstock; 10 © INSADCO
Photography/Alamy; 12, 23 © Florin Stana/Shutterstock; 13 ©
Rebecca Ashworth/Shutterstock; 14 © Mark Stosberg; 15 ©
www.dft.gov.uk/bikeability; 16 © Marcel Jancovic/Shutterstock;
17 top © Matthew Cole; 19 © Goodluz/Shutterstock; 20 ©
Ermolaev Alexander/Shutterstock

Series Editor: Eloise Macgregor
Series Designer: Alix Wood
Illustrations: Alix Wood

Dewey number 796.6
HB ISBN 978 1 4451 4427 6
Library ebook ISBN 978 1 4451 4432 0

Printed in China

Franklin Watts
An imprint of
Hachette Children's Group
Part of The Watts Publishing Group
Carmelite House
50 Victoria Embankment
London EC4Y 0DZ

An Hachette UK Company
www.hachette.co.uk

www.franklinwatts.co.uk

Contents

Hi!
I'm Safety Sam.
I'll help you learn
how to be safer on
your bike.

We love riding a bike

Riding a bike is fun and it keeps you fit and healthy. You can cycle to school or just for some time out with your family or friends.

Before you start cycling, make sure your bike is the right size for you and is in good working order. Always wear the right gear.

Make sure you cycle where it is safe. Never cycle on a busy road.

The best places to ride are on cycle tracks or pathways in parks and other places where there are no cars. How can you tell this is a special cycle track?

Ask Safety Sam

What do I need to take with me?

- Make sure you have a bottle of water with you, especially if you're going on a long ride and it's hot.

- Even for short rides in winter, if you're wearing thick clothes you can get hot and sweat a lot, so you need water to help keep you alert and **hydrated**.

What to wear

Most serious bike accidents are caused to the head and brain. Be smart and always wear a helmet. Wear bright clothes so you can be seen.

Buy a proper bike safety helmet from a bike shop and ask the salesperson to fit it for you. The helmet should not slip around when you turn your head. Keep the straps done up when you are wearing it.

BEWARE

Just because you're wearing a helmet doesn't mean you can cycle faster. Stay slow and keep safe.

Check that long scarves, wide trouser legs, skirts or coats can't get caught in the wheels. Wear shoes that fit well like trainers, not flip-flops or sandals. Make sure shoe laces are tied. Do a quick checklist with an adult before you set off.

Ask Safety Sam

Can I ride with my hood up?

- No. A hood muffles noise and you need to hear.

- A hood will block the view from the corners of your eyes.

- You need all your **senses** to ride safely.

Check out your bike

Give your bike a weekly check with an adult to make sure it's safe. Never ride your bike unless everything is in full working order.

Check that your seat, handlebars and wheels fit tightly. Oil your chain. Make sure your brakes work well and aren't sticking.

brake lever

handlebars

seat

brake

wheel

wheel

bike chain

Make sure your lights are working. If you want to ride your bike when it is getting dark, you should have a white light fixed on the front and a red light fixed on the back.

Ask Safety Sam

Is bike size important?

- Yes, you need a bike that fits! This means when you stand up straddling the seat, you can stand with your toes touching the ground.

- You should be able to turn the handlebars, reach the brake levers and change gear easily.

BEWARE

Check your tyres to make sure they have enough air in them. Your tyres should feel hard when you press them. If a tyre is flat you will find it hard to steer.

Roads and pavements

Riding on a busy road can be dangerous and not much fun. Only ride in the road if you are with an adult or older person.

Legally no one is allowed to cycle on the **pavement** but most police will allow children to, especially if you ride carefully. If the pavement is crowded, get off your bike and push it. This is safer for you and the **pedestrians**.

BEWARE

When riding your bike keep your eyes on the street ahead — look out for car doors opening, cars backing out of drives, or people stepping out in front of you or suddenly stopping.

Ask Safety Sam

Can I ride my bike to cross the road?

- If you need to cross a road, it's best to get off your bike and walk across at a proper crossing.

- Hold your bike firmly next to you and walk across the road.

- Don't run, but don't dawdle.

Riding on a cycle track

It is much safer and more fun to cycle on proper cycle paths and tracks, but you still need to be careful and stay alert.

Even if there are not many people about, don't race. Look out for wet leaves, **potholes**, puddles, stones and litter on the path that might make your bike wobble or make you fall off.

BEWARE

Watch out for joggers, dogs and other children playing who might run in front of you.

It is safest to go out cycling with your family but remember to keep your eyes on the road even when chatting.

Ask Safety Sam

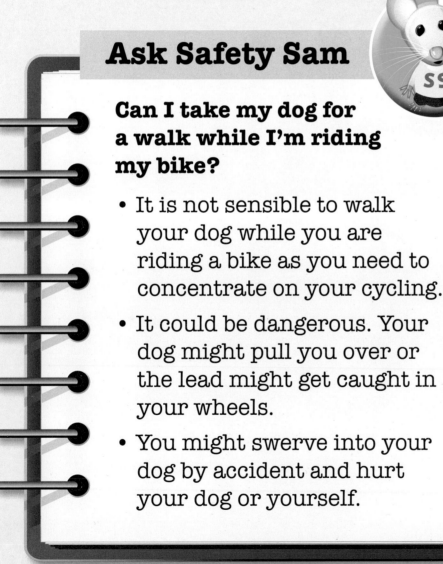

Can I take my dog for a walk while I'm riding my bike?

- It is not sensible to walk your dog while you are riding a bike as you need to concentrate on your cycling.

- It could be dangerous. Your dog might pull you over or the lead might get caught in your wheels.

- You might swerve into your dog by accident and hurt your dog or yourself.

Road rules

Before you go out cycling have some proper bicycle training by experts. This will teach you lots of new riding skills and make you feel more confident.

Signal clearly when you want to turn. Put your left arm out to turn left and your right arm out to turn right. Make sure you can be seen.

Use your bike bell to let other people know you want to overtake. Never ride your bicycle at anyone or at an animal or use your bell to frighten an animal.

BEWARE

If you stop at a shop, don't leave your bike lying on the pavement where it might trip up pedestrians.

Ask Safety Sam

How do I find out about bike training classes?

- Check out bikeability.dft.gov.uk.

- Ask at school, try your local council, check online or see if any of your friends or classmates have had training.

- Lots of organisations do school visits, so why not speak to a teacher about planning one.

Riding rules

Riding a bike is fun and exciting but bikes aren't toys and riding one is not a game.

'Don't try **wheelie** tricks in public places. If you want to do this, go to a proper bike park and wear shin pads and gloves. Don't carry a friend as a passenger or race with other friends.

Keep both hands on the handlebar at all times unless you're signalling so that you have more control of your bike if anything unexpected happens.

Ask Safety Sam

Can I wear my head phones?

- No. You need to be aware of what's going on around you all the time.

- If you're wearing headphones you won't hear if someone calls out a warning to you.

If you cycle to school, make sure you don't carry too many books, sports equipment, or large musical instruments that might make you wobble.

Cycling in the dark

Try not to ride at night or when it is dark. If you have to cycle in the dark make sure you are with an adult.

By law, at night your cycle must have its white front and red rear lights on. It must be fitted with a red rear **reflective** light. Placing **reflectors** on the front, the wheels and the pedals will help you to be seen as well.

If you have to go out when it is dark, plan your route so that you don't have to use any unlit lanes or paths.

BEWARE

If it is getting dark check your bike lights are working before you go out.

Ask Safety Sam

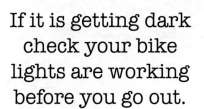

What's the best thing I can do to stay safe at night?

• Wear reflective or **fluorescent** clothing such as a jacket or reflective armbands or helmet.

• Decorate your helmet with your favourite reflective stickers.

Keep safe quiz

Answer the questions to find out how you can stay safe on your bike.

1. The best place to ride a bike is:
   a. The pavement
   b. Cycle tracks or pathways
   c. The road

2. If you have to cycle in the dark, make sure you:
   a. Have a torch
   b. Wear bright clothes
   c. Wear a reflective jacket

3. What's one of the most important things about your bike:
   a. It is the right size for you
   b. It has a basket
   c. It has a comfortable seat

4. The best type of shoes to cycle in are:
   a. Wellington boots
   b. Trainers
   c. Sandals

Safety Sam Says

Imagine you are cycling on a busy road. Why is it important to make sure you can see and hear what is happening all around you?

Glossary

bike chain A chain that transfers power from the pedals to the wheels of a bicycle.

brake A pad which presses on the wheel to help slow or stop a bike.

brake lever A lever on the handlebar that works the brake via a cable.

fluorescent A surface or colour that has a very bright appearance when light shines on it.

hydrated Having drunk enough water.

legally Being allowed by law to do something.

pavement A hard-surfaced path next to the road for people to walk along.

pedestrians People who are walking.

potholes Holes in a road surface caused by wear or bad weather.

reflective A surface that reflects light.

reflectors Small red discs or strips on a bicycle which reflect the light from headlights.

senses The physical abilities of sight, smell, hearing, touch and taste.

wheelie A bike trick where the front wheel is off the ground for a short time.

Answers from page 20-21
1) b 2) c 3) a 4) b

Further information

Books

Amstutz, Lisa J, *Bike Safety: A Crash Course*, Capstone Press, 2014.

Ruth Walton, *Let's Ride a Bike*, Franklin Watts, 2012.

Websites

Information on what to wear and road rules
roadwise.co.uk/children/road-safety/cycling

Fun games and quizzes to test your road safety
talesoftheroad.direct.gov.uk/cycling-safety.php

Every effort has been made by the publisher to ensure that these websites contain no inappropriate or offensive material. However, because of the nature of the Internet, it is impossible to guarantee that the content of these sites will not be altered. We strongly advise that Internet access is supervised by a responsible adult.

Index